THE SECRETS OF

BUILDING A GREAT ORGANIZATION

What your lawyer or accountant CAN'T tell you!

Written exclusively for:
Company Owners and CEOs of
privately owned businesses and professional practices

Bruce G. Clinton, MBA
Principlal
BusinessWise, LLC

P.O. Box 451, Madison, CT 06443-0451
Phone 203.458.1219
www.business-wise.com
bclinton@business-wise.com

ISBN: 978-06159094-2-4

TESTIMONIALS

"On very rare occasions, does a book come on the Market that adds the one idea or concept that will take a business to the next level of success. Bruce's book, 'The Secrets of Building a Great Organization' does exactly that. Implementing just a few of the strategies in Bruce's book will take your business to the next level."

Ken Varga, author of the book,
"How to Get Customers to Call, Buy and Beg for More."

"For businesses and really anyone running an organization, 'The Secrets OF Building A Great Organization' is a must read. It is full of fantastic, easy to understand solutions to challenges we all face everyday. If you adopt even just a few of the ideas you will see significant improvements in your organizations. I found this book fascinating and loaded with real commonsense facts and suggestions. The trick will be to get managers everywhere -including myself- to be honest about how we operate, so we can take the next steps to improve. Trust me, it's very good."

Anthony P. Rescigno
President
Greater New Haven Chamber of Commerce

"Thank you for thinking of me regarding sending me a copy of your book, The Secrets of Building a Great Organization. As I read the book, I found myself relating 100% to everything you said. The content was truly real-life/business, not just a bunch of theory. Your sub-title was absolutely perfect – 'what your lawyer or accountant CAN'T tell you.' Business owners have a lot to gain from reading your book. You should be proud of your work."

Steven Taback, President
Sandler Training/TEM

"All ambitious entrepreneurs and small business owners should read Bruce Clinton's new book, 'Secrets of Building a Great Organization.' It is a well-organized, clear and practical guide to building a strong business. As a former CEO of two advertising agencies, I wish it had been available when I needed it!"

**Wilder Baker, Principal
GPS for Management**

"As many savvy business people know, it's a real challenge to reduce a potentially complex subject into an idea that is presented simply, argued clearly and understood easily.

Bruce has done this rather *elegantly* and *eloquently* . . . with his book that is the basis for his consulting practice and speaking engagements with many businesses and charitable organizations.

This E-Book is especially attractive to charitable organizations who use Bruce and his E-Book as a 'value-add' for their donors who are owner / executives of small to mid-sized companies — especially those considered 'family-owned / operated' businesses."

**Bill Doerr, President
SellMoreMarketing**

"One thing I should tell you... I am brutally honest.
I loved the book; I believe it is high value and I want people I know to know you."

**Terri Levine
The Business Growth Guru**

"Congratulations again on your E-Book 'Secrets.' As I read through it I can clearly hear you saying all the tips, techniques, phrases, quotes, etc. You've taken all your pearls of wisdom and processes and put them to paper form. Great job!! It's an effective, highly practical, easy to understand and implementation-ready workbook and field guide. The challenge for the reading audience is to assess where they are, what they want/need and then commit to applying the solution(s); exactly as you've described. Leadership is a talent; and

the toughest person to lead is our self. It always starts at 'home.'
Best of luck with your 'authorship' career!"

Barry Foster, CRC, RCC, CPBA
Your Personal Success Guide

"In writing 'The Secrets of Building a Great Organization,' Bruce
Clinton has set forth a blue print for improving management through
simple evaluations, adjustments & actions. These lead to a positively
functioning team or company & great profitability."

Tom Tussing, Owner
Active Manufacturing

"I've gone through your book fully and like it. This type of practical
information is just what entrepreneurs need -- practiced business
people, too, but especially people who have never run a business
before. I'll be glad to make it available to others."

Deirdre Silberstein
Silberstein & Associates LLC

"I read your book last night - practical, immediately applicable
advice, very accessible but not at all simplistic. I could have used it
back when I was running the business - I would have hired and
managed better!
   I think this will be of particular value to family firms who are
struggling to develop a professional managerial structure - to rely
less on a rugged individualist entrepreneur, and broaden their non-
family management team. Most don't have the first clue as to how
to determine what skills and capabilities they need, how to interview
for them, and how to bring the new manager on board
successfully. I'm glad to have this excellent resource."

Amy
(Amy is a former CEO of a multi-generational family business and
former partner in an international law firm specializing in taxation
and founder of a family business consulting firm)

"Any current or aspiring business owner will find practical, do-able wisdom in Bruce Clinton's The Secrets of Building a Great Organization. Bruce clearly lays out the challenges of growing your business, provides ways of assessing your current practices, and offers very practical solutions. The content is rich, based on real-life situations, and is loaded with processes that you can implement - beginning today."

Millie Grenough, Executive Coach, Speaker
Author of OASIS in the Overwhelm

"I recommend this book to every business owner who wants to take their business to the next level. If you want to create a professionally customized working atmosphere for your employees, this book is your personal guide. The week after I read this book I used the interview skills from the book to re-interview a candidate I was about to hire. I learned effective questioning and new listening skills which allowed me to better get to know and understand the candidate (whom I did not hire). I believe I avoided 'The cost of the hiring error' tangible and intangible in chapter 5."

Bob Sisti, CLTC, Principal
PMG Insurance & Financial Services

"Bruce Clinton is a talented, gifted individual who has spent a lifetime trying to figure out how organizations function, how good ones differ from poor ones, and how to apply the lessons he's learned to improve the businesses he works with.

In his new book, *The Secrets of Building a Great Organization,* he distills the lessons of his 50-year career in a very practical, readable 70-page 'how to' manual. Starting with 'Stages of organizational growth' and ending with 'succession planning,' he goes through the HR, training, and organizational development functions need to build a staff a business.

The mid section is where the book is at its very best, showing Clinton's knowledge of how to define jobs, and hire and train employees and managers. He provides a number of very useful checklist, forms, and tactical guides. If you are a new manager starting out on your career, you will find this a very, very useful guide to the basic, essential 'blocking and tackling' skills of management. If you are an experienced manager, it will be a useful refresher—and you will probably learn a few new things, as well.

The book doesn't offer any magic formulas. He's the first to point out that there aren't any. But it does provide the tools that make the hard job a supervising and managing a lot easier.

Bob Brady, CEO
Business & Legal Resources (BLR, Inc.)

"I've spend my entire business career growing small, high tech, entrepreneurial enterprises into viable profit making organizations. I must tell you that "The Secrets of a Great Organization" provides the best roadmap I've seen for today's generation of managers to follow in building dynamic organizations in our challenging business environment. Thanks for writing this timely and useful book!"

Donald J. Moore, CEO
Harmonics Limited, Inc.

"My goal was to reach out with a thank you for your book this morning. I got quite off track - *I couldn't put it down.* I see that your background in psychology was an awesome pairing with your business education. Thank you also for your generosity in sending out the e-version of your book. There are people in my sphere I know will enjoy it immensely. Hopefully over time I will run into those that need your services."

Jodi Golub
Realtor

ADDITIONAL RESOURCES

EXCLUSIVE TO THE READERS

OF THIS BOOK

Because I believe in providing value and teaching others the basics of "Building A Great Organization," my team and I have put together additional chapters and resources to help small and medium business owners just like you get the most their leadership endeavors, as well as having a team of people who can help along the way.

We combine the many years of knowledge obtained from working with our clients to offer lessons of the experiences from many businesses and professional practices, as well as the success and lessons learned from applying the leadership models in my own business. From time to time, we will offer valuable information provided by other well-vetted professionals.

The additional information and resources include reports, audio CDs, videos, invitation to seminars, training, and more – absolutely FREE to our readers.

The additional resources are for business and professional practice owners who desire to grow or are growing and are experiencing the challenges of growth and succession. If you are looking to experience more fun and freedom while increasing you profit, then these resources are for you!

This information could be worth hundreds of thousands or even millions of dollars to you and your organization. To claim these additional resources, fill out the quick form on our website, www.BrucesGift.com, or call 203-458-1219. You'll start receiving this valuable information right away.

www.BrucesGift.com   (203) 458-1219

"Leadership is creating an environment in which people want to be part of the organization and not just work for the organization. Leadership creates an environment that makes people want to, rather than have to, do. It is a business imperative to create that environment. I must give purpose, not just work and function."

—*Horst Schulze, former COO, Ritz-Carlton hotels*

CONTENTS

DEDICATION

I do not walk alone in this journey. I'm blessed with my wife of 46 years, Susan, and five wonderful children: Heather, Stacy, Wendy, Derek and Courtney. All of them have always been supportive and understanding.

I've also had the fortune of being mentored by Paul Reinke and Jim Cornetet, the founders of Executive Consulting Services. Paul and Jim were pioneer consultants to privately owned businesses and had the unique ability to take the complex subject of management and leadership and develop timeless processes to develop management/leadership talent. They helped me to grow my real estate business and to understand the role of leadership and management. Later, when I sold my business, I was privileged to become a licensee. This helped me further my understanding of the unique aspects of growing an entrepreneurial business.

Last, but not least, I thank the hundreds of company and professional practice business owners and their thousands of managers, who, in the last 35 years, have honored me with their trust in my services and the services of my business owner advisory company, BusinessWise, LLC. Many of these business owners started as my clients and remained as lifelong friends. I am grateful to the hundreds of clients who have helped shape and sharpen my business expertise and improve my organizational development skills by giving me the privilege of serving their needs. My clients have taught me. I will always be grateful to them.

THIS IS THE BOOK FOR YOU IF...

CEO/owners of privately held companies and professional practices who will receive the greatest benefit from this book fit the following description:

- $1- $150 million in annual sales
- Approximately eight to 200 employees
- U.S. based
- Face growth or succession issues
- If family owned, the business owners and principals may not work well together but (there is trust, respect as a basis for communication among the family members)

Learning and applying the content of *Secrets Your Lawyer and Accountant Can't Tell You about Building a Great Organization* will enable these types of organizations to resolve many critical and common issues including:

- Overcoming communication breakdowns
- Creating stronger leadership
- Dealing with company members who have reached their level of incompetence
- Fitting family members into the business
- Retaining good employees
- Attracting highly qualified employee talent
- Providing depth of talent and an exit strategy to help pass the company on to new leadership
- Preparing the family's next generation to run the business
- Managing key stockholders who are no longer active in business but can be growth obstacles
- Building a workable succession plan

- Reversing a trend of lower sales among some long-term clients
- Adjusting pay scales appropriate to performance
- Distinguishing proper job roles among family business partners
- Removing the fear of sharing financial information among family members
- Aligning personal goals with business growth and profitability
- Improving sales performance

INTRODUCTION

Secrets Your Lawyer and Accountant Can't Tell You about Building a Great Organization (hereinafter referred to as *Secrets*) is about you and your organization: where it is, where it has been and ultimately where it could go. The purpose of this book is to assist you in identifying the professional skills that you will need to acquire to build a truly great organization.

The content in this book is based on more than 35 years of consulting work with owners of entrepreneurial businesses and professional practices. Many of these businesses were family owned. To attain organizational greatness, family owned businesses must meet a unique set of demands with a special set of dynamic skills and talents.

Secrets emphasizes the essential professional skills required to build, maintain, expand and perpetuate a great organization by working through people. The concept of greatness is based on recruiting and selecting the right people for the right positions, providing the practical knowledge and skills to perform their jobs well in a challenging environment and managing them to achieve consistent, efficient and quality results.

Lack of greatness is characterized by low and sporadic production, turnover, inferior leadership, poor use of time, slow or no growth, management by crisis, and devalued and underutilized people. Great organizations have learned how to provide outstanding products and services by maximizing their human resources through professional management processes.

Secrets includes action items. In order to get maximum benefit from the insights, tools and knowledge provided here, you will need to put the concepts presented here into action. Think about how to shape the concept of greatness to fit your organization's needs. We will consider the overall objectives in running an organization, but our emphasis will be on the underlying key to the success of any organization—its people. We will explore the five critical leadership skills:

> Recruiting
> Selection
> Development
> Management
> Motivation

We suggest you approach this book with an inquisitive and open mind. Compare your organization and its management/leadership practices to the concepts presented in *Secrets*. Think about how you can utilize and apply this information in your organization and you will obtain the greatest return for the investment of your time—the application of something you learned!

Relax and have fun with the concept of building a great organization. For the purpose of this book, we define management and leadership as:

Management—the planning, developing, controlling and maximizing of information, resources, money, time and technology to achieve predetermined and agreed upon objectives.

Leadership—the discovering, developing and empowering people to achieve their personal goals while achieving the organization's goals.

In simpler terms, we agree with how Warren Bennis distinguishes between leaders and managers. Bennis stresses that leaders are people who do the right thing; managers are people who do things right.

CHAPTER 1

THE STAGES OF ORGANIZATIONAL GROWTH

The logical place to begin our journey is to examine how privately owned businesses and professional practices grow. There is a natural and predictable set of stages into all companies fall.. Here we will cover the four major stages of business growth: Entrepreneurial, Personal, Organizational and Beyond.

The personal goals of the owners drive business decisions and ultimately form the basis of the growth stage where the business will reside. You do not need to attain a certain growth stage nor must you go through all these stages. You may start and indefinitely remain in the entrepreneurial stage. That is your choice and I place no value judgment on your conscious decision. That said, progressing through these stages is the surest and clearest path to greatness.

This chapter foreshadows what to expect as you expand your organization and build toward greatness. If you are frustrated or stuck in your growth cycle, this chapter may help explain why that is and what you can do to move forward to more fun and profits.

Take special note of the final stage of growth as described in this chapter. I call this stage, "Beyond." It's the growth stage of business perpetuation—an earned right. As you begin to grow into this stage, begin to plan for your exit. Start this process early to give your business and yourself the most options.

I have shared these stages with hundreds of company owners in seminars. As you read through them, think about your own company and its history. Identify which stages you have experienced and which stage your company is currently experiencing. You may discover that you thought you were in one stage of growth, but actually are functioning in another.

Entrepreneurial or Startup Stage: Generally a 1- or 2-Person Show

In this stage, the reason for your business may not be the best reason. Perhaps you started the business to challenge yourself, or because of your dissatisfaction working elsewhere or unfair treatment you received at your previous company. Many entrepreneurs establish their own practice or business because their old company goes out of business; there's no room for growth; they have a personality conflict; or they desire more dollars. Others in this stage want to prove themselves; can't work for anyone else; or don't like their former boss. The behavior of a company owner who operates in this development stage is easy to spot. You, as the entrepreneur, usually can be described as driven and as having an insatiable appetite for growth. Other common characteristics are: risk taker, skilled survivor, impatient, in need of new challenges, easily bored, demanding in the details he or she wants from others, intuitive, desiring recognition, aggressive, ambitious, innovative, charismatic, creative and energetic. To owners in this stage, loyalty means a lot and is an essential element in promotion decisions. ***But this can be your Achilles' heel. I'll explain why when we discuss the next stage.***

PERSONAL STAGE

Organizations in the personal stage have a founder who has built the first business universe with supplementary talent. Perhaps the company has expanded by adding administrative or sales support employees. In the beginning, communication is good; the owner hires compatible people, trains by imitation, leads by example and makes all decisions. This is fun. The company is charting new ground. Success depends on the entrepreneur. As the entrepreneur goes, so goes the company.

If your organization is well advanced in this personal stage, you're always looking to expand. You have to add staff rapidly to keep up with business growth. Once the head count or business universe grows to more than 10 or 12 people, the owner is obligated to create a new position—a manager—and turn over some responsibility and start delegating many more duties.

The decision to promote someone into a management role is based on rewarding a top producer who has demonstrated loyalty. Owners in the personal growth stage of their business demand loyalty and reward loyalty. Here's where this trait can be the company's Achilles' heel: The owner assumes this loyal employee is prepared to manage, but when things are not done correctly or the way he would do them, the owner jumps in to do the task himself In this way, the owner intentionally takes back the responsibility and undermines the new manager's authority.

Imagine a 500-pound parrot (they could really make a mess in their cage couldn't they?) taking command and undermining the manager by breaking down the chain of command. The beach ball of ownership expands to the point where the owner can hardly get his arms around it.

Choosing the wrong manager and then breaking the chain of command sets off a tragic series of events. A poor management selection decision will result in poor recruiting and selection of new staff. Training will be inadequate. There will be little or no supervision. Employees will sense a weak motivational environment.

At best, a strong economy may be robust enough to carry along an organization in this state. But the company is limited in growth because you—the owner— must make up for your poor management/leadership selection. **You have created a sterile hybrid— you cannot reproduce your organization or grow it.**

This is very frustrating. In the worst case scenario, the economic climate changes and you do not have the depth of talent to survive the business downturn. At the very best, the business will own you and steal your fun and enjoyment. The personal goals that drove you to start your business and to succeed at first are not being achieved.

> "Our chief want in life is somebody
> who will make us do what we can."
> —*Ralph Waldo Emerson*

ORGANIZATIONAL STAGE...WHERE BOTH FUN AND PROFIT CO-EXIST!

This phase of growth is characterized by the organization's ability to reproduce significant depth of leadership and management talent. In the organizational stage, there's a solid, healthy bridge between the owner and all employees. This bridge is the owner's ability to systematically select, develop and manage people capable of leading.

If your business has reached this stage, then you probably recognize that only one in seven top producers possesses the capacity to be a good manager or leader. In this stage, you will likely reward employee loyalty and job achievement, but not by blindly putting top producers into management roles. The latter is a mistake commonly seen in the *Personal Growth Stage.*

Your job at this stage is to build a team of autonomous leaders and this is quite challenging. But you know you can't make every decision and you value having good leaders, independent thinkers, around you. Your autonomous managers have authority and responsibility over people, production and profit as described in your written company policies and procedures. In the organizational stage, you create more formal business processes and learn how to develop leadership talent.

BEYOND...YOUR EXIT STRATEGY

This stage is not a given. It is an earned right. If you are the owner of a company in the Beyond stage, then you have the ability to transition away from the day to day business. You have a trained and capable team that can run the business profitably with or without you. You can retire or pursue other challenges. Organizations in the Beyond stage have many business models in place and a depth of leadership talent within the company. Many of the necessary talent development processes your company needs to meet the challenges unique to this stage will be developed in this book.

I have worked with many owners who have successfully achieved the Organizational Stage and are becoming somewhat unchallenged or bored in their own business. In this case, they have worked themselves out of the day-to-day operations or at least are in a position to make this transition. This is the signal to begin to plan your exit plan. The danger in being bored is that many owners like to be their chief problem solver and therefore need to create a problem to become active and needed.

Another aspect reflective of the current economic period is the shortage of capital, which means the days of cashing out of your business without continued risk and involvement have disappeared. A new view of a privately owned business is one of a retained family asset. This has made the Beyond stage a bit more complicated, requiring owners to build depth in leadership talent and to utilize a team of professionals to help develop and secure their succession plan.

CHAPTER 2

CHARACTERISTICS OF GREAT ORGANIZATIONS

It took 30 years for me to discover the following characteristics. I developed them based on my experiences in countless workshops with many groups of business owners and CEOs. I also studied successful work environments where these traits existed in companies run by my best clients. *And my mentor, Paul Reinke, taught me that fun and profits go hand in hand. Implemented properly, these characteristics provide an environment of fun and profit.*

If we examine the best organizations, what do we find?

Imagine you're in a scientific laboratory and before you are hundreds of high quality businesses and professional practices. As a scientist, your job is to carefully examine these companies and find the common characteristics that make them great or *the best of the best.* In some ways, I've been in that scientific lab for 30 years. Here's what I've discovered makes great organizations great.

Known business goals
Up-to-date employee benefits
Competitive compensation
Strong customer relationships
Regular performance reviews
Strong values and integrity
Talent depth at all levels
Problem solving ability
Good feedback systems (MIS)

Management depth
Good internal communications
Strong training programs
Clear job descriptions
Encourages fun at times
Highly productive people
Professional management/leadership
Minimal rumors
Management/leadership models

Technology plans in place
Quality products and services
Continuous growth
Perpetuation plan in place
Teamwork
Employee-management trust
Love for the customer
Policies and procedures in place
History of sustained profits

Marketing plan in place
Low employee turnover
Career paths and well defined roles
Clear mission and values
Positive attitudes among employees
Survival-ability
Love for the employee
A win/win/win philosophy

How do you look?

So how does your organization look? On a scale of 1 to 10, with 10 being excellent, rate yourself in these key characteristics of great organizations. There is a form on the next page for you to use. If you're serious about building a great organization, ask 3 to 5 other qualified people to rate your business on this scale. Then hold a candid discussion on the rankings.

SURVEY: HOW CLOSE TO GREAT ARE YOU?

Rate your organization from 1 to 10 in each of these categories. Be prepared to explain the rationale behind your rankings.

Characteristic of Greatness (1 = poor; 5 = average; 10 = great)	1	2	3	4	5	6	7	8	9	10
Known business goals										
Management/leadership depth										
Good internal communication										
Up-to-date employee benefits										
Competitive compensation										
Strong customer relationships										
Clear job descriptions										
Regular performance reviews										
Encourages fun at times										
Strong values and integrity										
Talent depth at all levels										

Characteristic of Greatness (1 = poor; 5 = average; 10 = great)	1	2	3	4	5	6	7	8	9	10
Highly productive people										
Professional management/leadership processes										
Problem solving ability										
Minimal rumors										
Good feedback systems (MIS)										
Management models										
Technology plans in place										
Marketing plan in place										
Quality products and services										
Low employee turnover										
Continuous growth										
Career paths and well defined roles										
Perpetuation plan in place										
Clear mission and values										
Teamwork										
Positive attitudes among employees										
Employee and management trust										
Survival-ability										
Love for the customer										
Love for the employee										
History of sustained profits										
Policies and procedures in place										
Clear mission and values										
A win/win/win philosophy										

Any item rated below 6 is a need that, if not corrected, is a real threat to your organization and is an opportunity if solved.

Any item rated 8 or above is an organizational strength, and needs to be reinforced and understood as an existing opportunity. Without reinforcement, the key strengths will not become a conscious part of your culture and will disappear or become a weakness rather than a competitive advantage.

Take action: What do you need to do to raise your score?

Take your time completing the "How Close To Great Are You?" form. Try to be as objective as you can. Do remember that no organization is perfect. Even great ones have some weak areas. When you believe you have as accurate a reading of your organization's rankings as possible, then prioritize.

Think about which areas have the greatest impact on your company's success. Spend the bulk of your time on those areas. Don't assume that strengths you have now will continue on forever. Make sure you have whatever it takes to keep your organization's best qualities as outstanding as they are today. For example, for Strong Customer Relationships, examine why your scores are high and examine what you do to develop these relationships and what key actions build relationships. You may even look at your best relationships and determine the characteristics of these customers. There are potential models to be developed.

Build a written plan as to how you will move toward greatness by moving up in these rankings. Make your plan S.M.A.R.T: Specific, measurable, achievable, realistic and time-bound.

Work on your organization's most vulnerable link

At what job level is your practice or company most vulnerable? Different experts will give different answers to this question. I believe the lowest level of your management or leadership team is your most vulnerable link. This team—often line managers—works closest to the client or end product. This is the point where the owner's vision, mission and values are passed on to the employees closest to your client or product. ***The ability of the line manager to recruit, select, develop, maximize and retain talent is paramount to building a great organization.***

Other ways to evaluate the strength of your organization

Additional indicators of strength are your Per Person Profit and Per Person Production and the number of strong managers/leaders you employ. If you have a large sales organization, rank each salesperson in order of their productivity over a similar time period. Let's assume you have eight sales people. Divide them into four quarters (quartiles), add up their personal productivity in each quartile and then divide their total production into each quartile to determine the percentage of the total they represent.

For example, assume there are eight salespeople and a total production of 800 units. The top quartile (two salespeople) produces 400 units. That means 50% (400/800) of the total productivity comes from the top quartile of the sales staff. If salespersons three and four (the second quartile) produce 250 units, then they account for 31.25% of total production (250/800). Combining the production of the top and second quartile shows that the top 50% of the sales force accounts for 82% of the productivity. Ideally, you want to see the sales production distributed more evenly over the total sales staff. A balanced production signifies depth in talent and that is a good way to be!

When you have depth in sales talent you will ideally see the productivity more evenly divided among the quartiles. If the top two quartiles account for more than 70% of the total, you may need to work on upgrading your sales team. This exercise can be done for any group of people who hold the same job position to get an indication of talent and performance depth.

"The best executive is the one who has sense enough to pick good people to do what needs to be done, and self-restraint enough to keep from meddling with them while they do it."
—Author unknown

The irony of building a great organization

In a privately owned business, all managers/leaders need to be better skilled in leadership processes—recruiting, selecting, developing and maximizing talent—than their counterparts in large publicly owned businesses. There are a couple of reasons for this. Privately owned businesses and professional practices don't have the resources that have been assumed by HR departments in larger companies. Often, the larger organizations forget these skills as their critical mass or size makes them seemingly unessential to their growth. In family-owned businesses, the people processes need to be more objective or they run the risk of placing a family member in a position where he/she will be detrimental to the success of the organization. The Bilco Company, a large privately owned family business, requires family members to apply for a position and it has been said by a key family member and executive that a family member may need to be more qualified than a non family member to gain a key position...

The balance of this book will cover the unique role of the CEO and the people systems that you will need in place to successfully build the depth of leadership necessary for sustained, profitable growth. We will also go over how to build the value necessary to transfer ownership to the next generation at the appropriate time.

CHAPTER 3

THE CEO POSITION DESCRIPTION

A great organization starts with a great chief executive officer. Great CEOs excel at delivering the two basic outcomes that this position demands:

Assures the survival, growth and perpetuation of the organization at a profit through a team of key managers and support staff
In a sales organization, meets or exceeds personal production goals

To deliver these two key outcomes, you, as an outstanding CEO, perform a variety of tasks and functions:

1. Recruit and select your team of managers and key support staff
2. Train your managers to recruit, select, train, manage and motivate their team
3. Manage your key people by evaluating regular periodic feedback and results and measure against predetermined and agreed upon objectives and standards
4. Motivate key people via personal goals, achievements and career paths
5. Establish a long-term business plan
6. Establish survival and growth plans in financial, people and market areas
7. Develop the structure and processes to achieve the organization's goals
8. Establish and monitor basic quantitative indicators in the areas of people, production and profit

9. Manage the fiscal affairs of the organization (budgets, lines of credit, investments, compensation programs, etc.)

10. Disseminate your management philosophy throughout the organization

11. Develop a mission and values statement

12. Select and develop your successor and perpetuation plan

13. Formulate and implement a management development program to meet your growth and perpetuation needs

14. Execute corporate social, civic and trade association responsibilities

15. Analyze market needs and oversee the development of products and services to fulfill these needs

16. Develop your area of personal production

> *"Accept the challenges, so that you*
> *may feel the exhilaration of victory."*
> —General George S. Patton

Survival is up to you alone

No one else in your organization has responsibility for survival of the organization. You will have all of your assets at risk at all times. ***You will be the last person paid when you're in the early stages of growth. During your career, the organization's survival will be at stake more than once. That is a reality of business. And it adds excitement to ownership.***

Growth is based on depth of leadership and talent

Growth will be your vision and dream in your early stages. As time goes on, you will build a leadership and management team that will not only contribute to the growth, but will bring forth new ideas. Growth must be continuous and profits need to be sustained to fuel the organization's future.

The most astute CEOs and owners seek strong talent. David Ogilvy built Ogilvy & Mather, one of the greatest advertising agencies of his time. When he appointed a manager to head a new office, Ogilvy would send the manager a Russian doll. Inside that doll was a smaller doll and inside that one was one smaller still—six dolls in all. Inside the smallest doll, Ogilvy would put this note:

> "If each of us hires people who are smaller than we are, we shall become a company of dwarfs, but if each of us hires people who are bigger than we are, Ogilvy & Mather will become a company of giants."

You want to hire the best so you will be challenged and stimulated.

Wise CEOs also learn that their team members need to achieve their goals as the organization and the owners achieve their goals. The search for win/win/win situations should never end.

Perpetuation (succession) is also your sole responsibility

This is your exit plan and the continuation of your business beyond your life span or interest span. It is the aspect of your career that will give you the most personal options and is often not planned for soon enough. If you implement the secrets of this book, you will have more personal options at the time of your exit.

Personal production

In many privately held companies, the owner wears an additional hat: personal production. Your personal production may be in sales, manufacturing or research and development. Keep contributing in your area of expertise as long as you can make significant contributions without neglecting your other CEO functions. But do learn to delegate responsibility and give authority to others as the company grows.

As a leader, you want to hire people smarter than you are to guide and grow different aspects of the business. Once you hire smart, you've only just begun. To hold onto the best employees and keep them motivated, continually give them opportunities to develop their leadership skills. Be certain your management team has the skills and knowledge to develop their teams. At all costs, you will want leadership processes that will assure your organization maintains a competitive advantage.

Build an organization that at all levels has the capacity to recruit, select, develop, maximize and retain talent. It is the number of quality people in all positions that will ultimately sustain your profitable growth and meet the challenges of the times.

CHAPTER 4

WHAT TOP PEOPLE EXPECT FROM MANAGERS AND LEADERS

*"The pessimist sees the difficulty in every
opportunity; the optimist, the opportunity in
every difficulty."*
—L. P. Jacks

Here are a few rules to consider when selecting someone to lead a team. You may view some of them as common sense, but don't let that fool you. My 30 years of experience with both great and poorly performing companies has convinced me these rules are not commonly practiced, yet they are extremely important for building greatness.

Give respect and trust

If you choose someone with a production role to become a group leader, you and your entire management team must give the new leader respect and trust. The new group leader's past achievements and successes will influence his/her success in this new role. This will be certainly true of all line managers you need to select. This is a given. But there are some behavioral characteristics that also need to be considered in addition to top performance and loyalty when identifying and choosing a team leader or manager. Think about the best leaders you have known in your business career. I believe you will find the following three characteristics accurately describe them:

1. Professional—knows how to select talent

The best leaders know how to select talent for their team. They are good trainers and develop the job skills and abilities of their people. They know how to hold employees accountable to stated objectives and they also know how to provide a positive motivational atmosphere. They are skilled at professional management and leadership.

2. Available when needed

Great leaders are available when needed. These leaders have a sense of timing and are readily available during tough times or times of critical need. They don't run away from problems. They do believe problems are opportunities in disguise.

3. Understands each individual

The best leaders understand each individual's needs and work style. They are aware of individual goals and strive to help individuals meet their goals as the business meets its objectives. They know that no employee is perfect and they work perfectly well with all types of employees.

Unique behavioral characteristics found in top managers/leaders

1. A need to lead

Great leaders have a burning desire to see others grow and learn. Natural line managers or leaders have the ability to sublimate their ego for the benefit of others. They are willing help team members break their own personal sales record.

2. A need for power

These leaders are comfortable with and seek out responsibility. They have the ability to take charge, pursue problems, hold people accountable and make unpopular decisions. This is the "iron fist" within the velvet glove.

3. A need for people

Top managers/leaders want to be around people. They respect others and want to see them succeed. They understand and listen to others. They earn trust. They know when to push and prod and when to compliment and ask. This is the "velvet glove" **of people sensitivity**.

CHAPTER 5

SELECTING THE TALENT: THE BEGINNING, OR THE BEGINNING OF THE END

*"There is something that is much more scarce,
something rarer than ability. It is the ability
to recognize ability."*
— *Robert Half*

The cost of a hiring error

Selection errors cost four to five times annual salary. Hire the wrong person for a $30,000-a-year job and it eventually will cost you about $150,000. The tangible costs alone of a poor hire are often quoted as a minimum of 25-35% of a year's base salary. The costs go beyond direct salary and benefits. The costs can include materials, recruiting expenses (fees, travel expenses, management time, and advertising), training time and training materials. Other less obvious costs could be losses such as spoilage of materials, products or other resources, lawsuits and even the loss of a customer. All of these costs are quantifiable, and you probably can think of more. And not the least of costs is the time and effort to repeat your recruiting and selection process and training.

Intangible costs of a poor hire are five times the tangible costs

Intangible costs are not as easy to quantify. Here are a few that other company owners have shared with me:

Loss of company reputation

      Loss of potential clients and referrals
      Loss of employee morale
      Loss of team productivity
      Loss of credibility with other team members

One poor hire can also cause the turnover of productive team members. Remember, people join a company, but they tend to leave a poor leader or manager. When I facilitate a discussion of average turnover costs with company owners, we never reach a total cost of less than $8,000 in tangibles and $40,000 in intangibles.

Selecting the wrong manager is worse

Worse than poor hiring decisions are poor management selection decisions. Select a poor manager and your turnover costs are the number of people managed times the average cost per turnover.

Time and time again, I have witnessed the loss of an office or that entire profit center because there is a poor manager or leader in place. In the case above, if the team has eight members and we assume that they produce a million dollars of revenue, then losing this unit is a million dollar loss! This is only the "opportunity cost" for each year.

The question I often ask CEOs and business owners is: How much do you budget for staff turnover? They always answer, "We don't." My follow up question is, "Where does this loss appear?" The answer is: "From bottom line profit."

My own real life success story

Do you wonder how the selection process you're about to discover works in real life? Wonder no more. Before I learned and implemented the selection process outlined here, I ran a sales office with 32 part-time and full-time employees. By making a decision to use this process, I doubled my sales with a much leaner staff of just 12. A commitment to hiring only high quality team players who were the right fit and could produce made a huge difference in the success of my business

Great talent isn't retained without this.

When I conduct organizational studies, part of my process is for all managers to write their perception of their job by listing their key activities. Having read hundreds of these responses, I'm sad to report that there's no reference to staffing their team and no reference to recruiting as an activity. Great talent is not going to be retained if management does not recognize recruiting and selecting great talent as a key leadership activity.

The bottom line is that when you select great talent, your organization will grow and prosper. When you do not, you end up with morale issues, lower production, slower growth and lower profits long term. Selecting great talent also gives you more options at the time of succession due to the depth of talent within your organization.

The right person in the right position will be a great asset. The right person in the wrong position will be a detriment to the organization's success. The right person in the right position is easily trained, develops naturally and will accomplish the job objectives.

The six common selection errors

One of the sad outcomes of my consulting work is that I've seen, again and again, how companies make the same mistakes in selecting employees. There are a few common errors made by a majority of companies. ***Here are the top six selection errors that you need to avoid.***

1. Subjectivity over objectivity
Using your gut to find great talent is fine as long as you gather facts (objective information) to confirm your gut feelings. A Harvard study revealed that the use of interviews only as a means for selection were successful 14% of the time. I bet you have experienced a quick

hiring decision based on gut feeling that resulted in poor performance or poor chemistry for the organization.

2. Making hasty decisions
There are tendencies, in over 63% of selection interviews, to make the hiring decisions in the first four minutes of the interview. Don't do this. It takes 90 minutes of a patterned or structured interview to get to real behavior. Many professional recruiters suggest that you not form any judgments in the first 30 minutes. If you do, you are in danger of missing out on potentially good candidates who do not interview well, or worse, hiring a poor fit because of the candidate's ability to interview well.

3. Accountability for selection errors
An even worse selection error is made when managers don't view selection as an important job responsibility. This occurs often in companies that do not train their managers in this critical leadership task.

4. Lack of good information on candidates
At BusinessWise, we have learned that interviewing alone is ineffective. The best selection processes include many tools like checking references, performing sample job tasks and conducting a second interview. Reference checks are often not performed and when they are, companies usually only verify information like employment dates. Most resumes are marketing tools—they often exaggerate accomplishments. In my experience, many times recommendations are positive because the person doing the recommending is hoping to move an underperforming employee out.

5. Untrained management
Make this error and it will lead to an organization that perpetuates degradation of talent. In other words, if someone is a 10/10, he or she will hire at best 9/10. The 9/10 will at best hire an 8/10. Over time, this erodes the depth of talent. Strong talents (10/10) will not remain in an organization when they are hired by 5/10 managers. ***People do not leave jobs—they leave unskilled and poor leadership.***

6. The wrong people are doing the hiring
In large organizations, you often find the wrong people are selecting new hires. Human resources sends the line manager poor talent. The manager and his team can't get the job done because the unit's not fully staffed or capably staffed and the manager doesn't have the time to interview and train. This catch-22 thrives when team leaders don't regard employee selection of talent as their responsibility. The talent problem gets compounded when HR departments cut back in difficult times.

Key ingredients of a successful selection process

When you commit to avoiding the six common selection errors outlined above, you're ready to build a great selection process. Here are the basics.

- **Compatibility with hiring manager, work group team and client.**
  You don't just want the most intelligent or most well educated or even the most experienced new hires. You want a person who will work well with your existing staff and within your company's culture. You can predict compatibility by looking for evidence of shared values. We all know of examples where someone can do the job technically, but who destroys a team and is problematic with many clients. We also know what it is like to work with and to anticipate interactions with someone you do not like or respect.
- **Fit to the position requirements**
  Measure all job candidates by their ability to do the job for which you are hiring. Do they have the skills or capacity to learn the necessary tasks? Do they have the talent or experience needed to perform the key requirements of the position?
- **Long-term staying power**
  Don't hire someone who doesn't seem likely to stay with your company. Ask yourself: Will the person still be here once we've invested our training and development time?

Will this candidate be a profitable and productive long-term team member? Sometimes people are just desperate for a position. Once they are hired they have only one foot in the door as they continue looking for what they see as a more ideal job.

• **Objective selection process**

Without an objective process, you are inclined to make a decision too early and on terms that may not be predictive of success in the position. Sticking with a disciplined selection process assures senior management that excellent talent is consistently being recruited and selected. Creating a complete and objective selection process requires an investment of time up front. That time is well spent because it will prevent the treadmill of turnover that consumes more time and steals from your bottom line profit.

• **Determine if the hiring manager can lead and manage the candidate**

We have witnessed managers hiring uncoachable and unmanageable people. Doing so makes the leadership job impossible. It becomes very stressful for the manager because he/she begins to lose credibility with the balance of the team. Credibility is obtained by the hiring manager leading the candidate through a disciplined process that will require cooperation and candid inputs. Also, there is a comprehensive interview designed to eliminate role play and reveal real behavior.

• **Determine if the candidate "can do" and "will do" the job**

I'm sure you've seen people who are "over their heads" in a certain job. There are key aspects of the job that are counter to their learning style or natural behavior. This is an example of "can't do." A good selection process would have identified this person as someone who can't do that particular job and the person would never have been hired. In the case of "won't do," you may find people who are performing well on the job— perhaps progressing nicely—who change their careers mid-stream. As an example, think of the salesperson who becomes an accountant or the trained accountant who becomes very successful in sales. These are examples of "won't do." They are more than capable of performing the position requirements and can be successful, but they leave or turn over because they are not engaged in the activities of the position. The "will do" match of the person to the position is absent. The selection process we will overview here uses a combination of processes: job definition, interviewing skills, assessments and references that ensure that you hire people who "can do" *and* people who "will do."

Begin with excellence

The cornerstone to building a great organization is using an effective recruitment and selection process. You are about to learn one.

Overview: *Earlier we discussed what was essential to build a great organization. Certainly your ability as an owner to develop a means to attract, appropriately place, develop, maximize and retain depth in talented people will not only sustain and grow your organization profitably...it will give you the most value and options when you are choosing your exit strategy.*

Truly, the recruitment and selection of great talent is the beginning of your organization's climb to greatness. With poor selection, you are at the beginning of the end of your organization. People who are well selected will be easy to train and lead and will add profits to the organization. They will be a key reason that you will have fun in your business.

People poorly selected are a drag on your company. We all know what it's like to work with people who are untrustworthy, unqualified or unproductive. Yet some privately owned companies choose to place someone in a job just because they like that person and have respect for him or her. This tendency leads to putting people in jobs where they will underperform and hurt the organization. These situations are tough. This poorly selected but respected person may be a friend or a relative or someone you rewarded for their loyalty or their production in a different job. As a leader, you cannot allow poor performance to continue indefinitely just because you like the person. If you do, how do you think the other productive members of your team will feel about your leadership?

The steps I outline here for the process of recruiting and selecting talent will go a long way toward preventing many of the people problems found in most organizations. This process is a discipline. It takes time. But it mitigates the time and cost of replacing a turnover. Just think about the $20,000-plus cost for each hiring mistake.

Define the position: You need to know what you are looking for

Begin by defining the position. Once you define the major measurable outcomes and key supporting activities the job requires, you'll be able to define the hard skills—the experience and education required for success. The soft skills are the talents and chemistry required to perform key job functions. To define these soft skills, look at your best performers in similar positions. Define what key functions they perform successfully and then identify the personality traits that these top performers have in common. Once you have defined the hard and soft skills that are keys to success, use these to measure the degree of fit of each candidate. If you have not defined the position, you are simply going through the motions of selection as you are not measuring objective criteria of fit.

As an example of this process, I will share what a multi-office real estate firm did to define the top three or four characteristics of their best producers. At this firm, 10 managers listed the top characteristics of their best sales people and then ranked the top five. They discovered a common thread. Every manager agreed that work ethic was the number one characteristic.

Closer examination revealed that all of the top producers were first generation of immigrated parents who came to the U.S. with virtually no assets. By defining key characteristics of top producers and identifying where they originated, the real estate managers agreed upon key areas for matching candidates to the position requirements. They also developed ideas for recruiting candidates.

Another process I use with larger clients incorporates the use of an assessment that measures learning style, work related behaviors and interests. We first look at people performing the same position for over a year. We pick a couple of clear objective performance indicators and then rank all the incumbents (assume there are 20 people doing the same job), with the top producer as 1 and the bottom producer as 20. We then assess the top five and the bottom five and determine how the assessment patterns differ (and they will). From the common areas that differentiate the top producers from the bottom, we are able to develop a Job Pattern to use when comparing candidates. This is a process of quantifying key soft skills that predict success in a specific position in your work environment.

Success story: defining the position pays off

A commitment to quality really works. A technology company needed to bring on a key executive into a CFO/Operations Manager role. The job required skills in accounting and outsourcing. The company needed to find better manufacturing options for new product enhancements. Both the accounting and outsourcing areas were out of control, as the incumbent staff and leadership had been outpaced by the business growth and challenges. A firm was contracted to perform a retained search for this key position. BusinessWise, working with ASearch, their retained executive search arm, formulated a position development team (PDT) consisting of the new executive's peers, incumbents performing the current job function and the CEO.

We took the PDT through a series of assessments and debriefed them on their thinking and behavioral styles, values and interests. This developed the ground work for better individual and team understanding. Next we had the PDT complete an online survey about the organization and the position. BusinessWise then consolidated all inputs, brought the selection team together and developed consensus on the position requirements. After a healthy discussion of organizational needs, we:

- Narrowed the position to five major responsibilities
- Assigned percent of time allocated to each responsibility
- Outlined the required and desired experience and education
- Set the compensation range and the next 30-, 60-and 90-day goals
- Determined achievement evidence for the goals

We also obtained commitment from the selection team on how they would support the new hire. Lastly, we went back to the assessments and redefined the soft skill indicators to reflect how the new hire would be similar and different from other team members. In essence, we had quantified the hard and soft skill requirements of the position. Everyone then knew what was needed in the new hire. People on the team who would be managed by this new person realized why a new person with specific talents was necessary for the business to move forward.

The right person was hired and within his first year, he had brought a million dollars of savings to the bottom line. This would not have been possible without going through the discipline of defining a position before we had tried to select people to fill it.

Recruiting candidates

A selection process does not function without two or more candidates. You must have a pool of candidates from which to choose. Without two or more good candidates, you only have a hiring process, not a selection process. This is why great leaders will constantly identify candidates for their team. When good candidates are plentiful, the manager/team leader will never be overwhelmed by unforeseen turnover or held hostage by employees who underperform.

All your team leaders need the authority and responsibility to recruit talent. Selecting talent is a fundamental skill at the line manager level. Besides, it's far too expensive to pay recruiting services for filling entry level positions.

Candidate Philosophy

The backbone of the recruiting process is *The Candidate Philosophy*. This is based on the fact that the best potential candidates for most positions are currently employed and likely content in their current position, We have learned by polling managers and owners that when asked if they experienced at least mild dissatisfaction in their current position in the last 12 months, more than 90% indicated they had experienced some form of dissatisfaction. Because of this, we realized that we should be proactive and approach people we felt were potentially a good fit for our organization. When we approached them, we asked if they would be willing to explore an opportunity together without any obligation on our or their part. This was the birth of *the candidate philosophy.*

Center of influence recruiting

One successful recruiting strategy for the line manager is Center of Influence recruiting. In this recruiting method, you identify people who know and have influence over possible candidates; who respect you; and who value the job opportunities within your organization. These individuals become your centers of influences (C of I). The C of I can be leveraged to identify candidates for you. People brought to you by a C of I tend to be more qualified than applicants.

Recruit continuously

Part of the high value of having a C of I is that good ones enable you always to be looking for good job candidates. Don't wait until you have an opening to begin recruiting. Always be looking for great talent. Recognize that almost everyone goes through a period of mild dissatisfaction yearly and therefore you can approach anyone who may be a good fit in your organization to explore an opportunity. Presenting the job opportunity to someone who's already employed gives you both time to consider objectively the degree of match between the candidate and your organization.

Don't be typical. Typically, managers wait until they need to hire someone and then start the process. Recruitment of great people is a continuous process. So is recruiting for sales positions. Great leaders keep their pipeline of candidates full and are constantly upgrading their team as they grow. *Recruiting talent is a fundamental part of leadership that is often overlooked, unless owners take the necessary step to make it a requirement of all leadership positions*.

The screening interview (aka The Thread of Success)

This interview is the first interview. It should last 30 to 45 minutes. The objective is not to make a hiring decision. With the screening interview, the only decision you are making is whether to continue keeping this person in your selection process. To do this, use the screening interview to determine if the candidate's past job experiences illustrate the skills and behavior that meet your position requirements. At BusinessWise, we call this a "thread of success." In order to accomplish this goal, you will need to know that the person is not likely to change his style and values, and that his past is going to be a strong indicator of his future.

I have developed three or four questions my clients use to uncover evidence of the "thread of success." The questions range from easy to difficult. The easy questions are from the candidates' past positions (and current position). The questions reveal what they liked or disliked about each job. In the next phase of this interview, you ask them to identify some of their achievements. The final phase gets them to explain in detail what they did or how they accomplished each individual achievement. You want to learn about what they've done in the past to determine if they used the behaviors and skills they would need to be successful in your company's position. The keys here are the specific examples—the details of how they succeeded and specifically what they personally achieved. Don't focus on general achievements or achievements that could be the result of people other than your candidate.

At the end of this initial interview, if you sense the candidate may be a good one, give the candidate a brief sell on how the opportunity with your company may meet his or her needs. Ask the candidate if she would like to continue exploring the opportunity. If the answer is yes, describe the next selection step. This next step should be an assessment or behavioral predictor, as I'll describe later.

Screening interview action plan

Objective: For this initial interview, your objective should be to uncover the *Thread of Success* that is necessary for success in the open position in your environment.

Timetable of screening interview: approximately 30 minutes

Method:
• Set ground rules. Explain your candidate philosophy, indicate that their information is confidential and ask permission to ask questions.

• Ask questions. Sequence your questions from easy to hard to difficult. Talk 20% of the time; listen about 80% of the time. Move your questions from general information to specific. When you ask for specific information and examples, then the questions become more difficult to answer, especially for the weaker candidate.

• Start with easy warm-up questions such as: What did you like about your most recent job? What didn't you like? Gather likes and dislikes about each past job and also the candidate's college experiences. With each answer, ask why or what caused the candidate to feel that way. Ask for examples.

• Move on to hard questions like: Tell me about a recent job success; in terms of your work, what are you most proud of; and what do you view as your greatest work achievements? You can ask about college if they don't have work experience. Let them go where they want to with their answers. Get a couple of specific examples.

• Finally, ask some difficult questions. You might refer them back to one of their stated achievements and ask them what they specifically did on that project or during that event. Gather as much detail and specifics as you can. Then, if necessary, do the same for the second achievement. As they are giving examples, compare what they have done to what is necessary for success on the job at your company.

• If you think they have a Thread of Success and you would like them to continue in the process, then give them a brief sell on your company. You might tie in the things they enjoy doing to the job opening you have. For example, if they've expressed an interest in learning about new products, you might be able to point out that your company introduces new products every three months. At the end of this screening interview, ask if they have any questions.

• Ask them if they would like to continue as a candidate. Describe the next steps in your selection process and ask if they would like to continue the process.

• If they do not fit your company or your job, exit them early. Describe how they may not enjoy your opportunity based upon their likes and dislikes.

Four keys to effective interviewing

1.   Past performance is the best indicator of future performance. As a person has been in the past, so he or she is likely be in the future.
2.   People speak in omissions and deletions. Listen for and try to have the candidate fill in any gaps you notice.
3.   Gather real-life examples from the candidate's past to verify behavior.
4.   Ask questions in sequence. Move from easy to difficult questions.

One highly successful company, PPS in Jacksonville, Florida, focuses on these five personality characteristics when they interview job candidates. Over time, they discovered that these five are good gauges of success in their organization.

1. Assertor: Is the person a doer?
2. Persuader: Can the person persuade a customer?
3. Values: Is the person honest and trustworthy?
4. Relator: Does the person get along with others, and can he or she build long-term relationships?
5. Ego: Does the person have self-regard and a high confidence level?

Source:
www.inc.com/magazine/19911201/6167.html?partner=newsletter_Sales

Behavioral predictors

After the screening interview, the next step (if you have decided to continue with a candidate) is a behavioral predictor or assessment tool. These tools resemble written questionnaires. How candidates answer the questions reveals more about their values, personal characteristics and what their behavior is likely to be in the future. Assessments are supplements to good interviewing processes and help you remain objective. They also reveal additional information for you to explore and they can further validate information that you have already gathered. A good assessment will have current reliability and validation studies and will be normative (measuring certain characteristics against the population).

The better assessments have a distortion factor that measure how honest and candid the candidate's responses are. The better assessments compare current job candidates with the patterns of behavior found in successful people performing the same job. Some assessments can be customized for your organization. The information that you receive from a good assessment would take six months for you to observe on the job.

I always caution BusinessWise clients not to rely too heavily on any one aspect of the selection process. Don't hire based only on a great screening interview or on a good score on the assessment tool. The assessment tool will give you plenty of insight on what a job candidate will and won't do on the job. It's also more objective than information gathered in an interview. But the behavioral predictor or assessment should account for 20 to 30% of your hiring decision. Use a selection process with many different candidate evaluations—the screening interview, an assessment tool, the reference check, the comprehensive interview and more.

Use the assessment tool early in the selection process. It will highlight areas that you may want to explore more fully later in the selection process. And administering the assessment tool is one of the least expensive steps in selection. A good assessment tool can also be used as an important feedback mechanism for upper management.

I'll explain how to validate an assessment as part of the next step in the selection process: The Comprehensive Interview. If you do not currently use an assessment tool, BusinessWise often recommends the online PXT Assessment.

Conducting the Comprehensive Interview

Let's review. You have taken the candidate through a couple of key steps. You have recruited the person and asked him to become a candidate, conducted a screening interview and found a thread of success that may be transferable to your opportunity. You have asked the candidate, after a brief sales presentation of your company, if he would like to continue to explore an opportunity together. Once this fact was confirmed, you set him up for the next step: to complete as assessment tool like the PXT Assessment.

If the assessment results meet your expectations for the open job, set up the Comprehensive Interview. This is a commitment that can take 90 to 180 minutes. Notify the candidate to be prepared to spend up to three hours on your site.

Comprehensive Interview Objectives

- Get to know the real behavior of the candidate
- Get his or her reaction to stress
- Make a conditional decision to hire
- Determine "can do" and "will do"
- Evaluate compatibility with you
- Determine if you can lead and manage the candidate

There are seven major components of the comprehensive interview:

1. Validation of the PXT or other assessment
2. Life Story Question
3. Patterned Interview Questions
4. Brief Personal Sell and Take Away
5. Exploring Areas of Concern
6. Trial Close
7. Set Up for the Expectations Meeting

On the next few pages, I have broken each section of the comprehensive interview into its own action plan. Remember, anytime that you know this person is not a "good fit" for your organization, you need to terminate the interview process.

VALIDATION OF PXT ASSESSMENT

Objectives:
- Set the ground rules for the interview
- Validate the PXT assessment
- Get to know the real person

Timetable:
15 to 30 minutes

Preparation:
- Read through the PXT and underline four to six statements that are positive about the person and positive for the position.
- Number the positive statements, with the most positive statement # 1 and second most positive statement # 2 and continue for all the statements selected.
- Set up the appointment for the interview.
- Make sure that you have allocated time in a private atmosphere (no phone calls, texts or other interruptions).

Conducting the interview:
1. Verify the time that the candidate allocated. Reschedule if not enough time is available.
2. Tell the candidate she can take notes and that you will be taking notes. Let her know that asking questions is okay but you may have to defer your answers to later time. Provide water. Sit at a round table, if possible. Make things comfortable but not overly comfortable. The atmosphere must be business-like.
3. Start the interview. Tell the candidate you are going to share the assessment results with her. Read the most positive statement first and ask, "Does this sound like you?"
4. Upon affirmative answer, ask them to share a specific example illustrating this behavior. If the example is unclear, ask for another example.
5. Continue using the same process until all the selected statements are validated.
6. Use this statement as a bridge to the Life Story Question: "Thank you for sharing that. I want to ask you to do something perhaps for the first time—I would like you to share your life story—hitting the points that were significant to you. Do not be afraid to brag." (Ask college students to begin their story with their first year of high school.)

LIFE STORY QUESTION

Objectives:
- Conduct an ongoing validation of behavior
- Assess candidate's fatigue factor

Timetable:

20 to 40 minutes

Methods:

1.   Start with something like: "So tell me about you. Share with me the high points of your life. Don't be modest; don't be afraid to brag. You can begin by telling me about your first year in high school."

2.   Slow down when a time period is skipped. Stay in area until you feel you have the whole story. Don't assume. Layer and probe to build a complete understanding.

3.   End with, "Thank you for sharing that. It was very interesting."

4.   Now go on to Patterned Interview Questions by saying, "I would like to ask you a few questions."

PATTERNED INTERVIEW QUESTIONS

Patterned Interview Question Objectives

- Evaluate if the candidate can do the job
- Evaluate if the candidate will do the job
- Determine if you can manage this person
- Predict compatibility with you and the team
- Determine key points for the specific sell

Timetable:
>30 to 60 minutes

Methods:
1. Use probing and layering to elicit specific rather than general statements.
2. Start asking questions:
    - "Tell me about some of your prior successes that would be meaningful to our position."
    - "What has been your relative standing as compared to others in school, projects and in the workplace?"
    - "How has what you have done up to this time made you qualified for our position?"
    - "What are you bringing to the table as requirements for top performance in this position?"
    - "What do you think will be the most difficult part for you working for our organization in this position?"
    - "What are your strong points?"
    - "If we were to ask your past supervisors what they had suggested you improve, what would they say?"
    - "What are your goals: short term, mid term and long term?"
    - "What makes you sense that you are a leader?"
    - "What has been your most difficult achievement to date?"
    - "What is your action plan if you do not get this position?"
3. Make a tentative decision to continue on in hopes of hiring.
4. Bridge to the next step in the selection process, the personal sell.

PERSONAL SELL

Objective: To paint a personal picture of the candidate enjoying and prospering in the job based on his or her specific needs.

Timetable:
>5 to 10 minutes

Methods:

> **Preparation:** Where to find information for a brief, powerful and specific sell:
>
> 1.   Notes from questions on likes and dislikes of past jobs
> 2.   Notes on their successes and personal strengths
> 3.   Notes on their interests
> 4.   Notes on their long-term goals

Presentation or Personal Sell:

1. Thank them for being candid and sharing information. Tell them that now is the time for you to share some information about our opportunity.

2. Verify that what you think you heard them say is important to them is actually what they value. Say something like, "You indicated that…was important to you."

3. Paint a picture showing how those important features can be met in your company in the open position.

4. Ask if they have any unanswered questions.

5. Ask them how they feel about the job opportunity now. If they're still interested, begin a discussion of any areas of potential concern or incompatibilities.

EXPLORING POTENTIAL AREAS OF CONCERN

Objective: Get their reaction to stress, take back control of the interview while exploring legitimate 2-4 areas of concern.

Timetable:

> 10 to 15 minutes

Preparation:

1. Review areas of the PXT Placement Report in which the candidate was not positive about the job. This could be a strength carried to an extreme or a place where they have fallen outside of the pattern in a behavior or vocational interest. An example of this may be their strengths in vocabulary may limit their ability to communicate with less skilled people.

2. Also look for concerns raised during the personal history, answers to likes or dislikes of past positions, patterned interview questions or information from reference checks from past supervisors or other people.

Method:

1. Bridge by telling them what you are going to do: "There are many aspects about your background that make you a very good fit for our company. However, there are a couple of things that may hinder your success with us. May I share those things with you and get your comments?"

2. Share each item one at a time. Then be silent and ask, "How would you handle that situation or how would you deal with this?"

3. Get their answer. Don't interrupt or fill silence. You may need to probe for an example of how they dealt in the past with this concern. Take detailed notes.

4. When all of the items have been shared and assuming that their answers are satisfactory, ask: "If I were to give you an offer now, what would your reaction be?"

5. Discuss any doubts they may have. Ask the closing question again. If favorable, bridge to expectations interview.

6. If they have accepted your job offer, say, "That is great. The next step and final step in our process is for both of us to define our expectations for what will make this a good opportunity for both of us and share those expectations at our next meeting." If the candidate is close enough to return on a different day, this final step should be done at a separate meeting. If the candidate has traveled a distance, take a break. Use the break to allow him to reflect. Then conduct the expectations interview within a half hour. Ideally, you would bring back the best candidates in order of your ranking (best first.)

EXPECTATIONS INTERVIEW

Objectives:
- Clarify the position expectations
- Understand what is important to the candidate
- Clarify next steps
- Make offer

Timetable:
         60 to 90 minutes

Preparation:
- Candidate outlines his or her expectations for a good relationship
- Hiring manager outlines his or her expectations

Method:
1. Exchange expectations
2. Assure candidate she or he is a good fit
3. Answer all questions
4. Reach agreement on expectations
5. Share job responsibilities and other specifics
6. Get candidate's agreement to all job requirements
7. Agree upon compensation and start date
8. Reiterate your expectations
9. Ask for the candidate's commitment and agreement
10. Welcome him or her to your team

The secret to growth and sustained profits

You have just reviewed a comprehensive selection process that can be implemented at all levels of leadership and management. Following the process is an essential element if you want to grow into a great organization. Master this process and the balance of the skills we will discuss will be easily implemented. That's because you will have recruited and selected team members that fit the position requirements and the chemistry of your team. ***Truly, you now have the secret to growth and sustained profits.***

CHAPTER 6

TRAINING: DEVELOPING HIGHLY PRODUCTIVE PEOPLE

To reach organizational greatness, you must continually develop talent. That takes a good training program. I've observed many poor training programs and I've made my own training errors. Let my battle scars and my 30 years of observations help you avoid making the following common training mistakes. We'll also cover some key training concepts.

There are three different phases of training or development your team members need to receive to become fully developed and reach their potential. All your managers should become skilled in all three phases.

Phase 1: Orientation training

New employees need to know the basic information about their position and how that position interacts with others in the organization. They need to understand the clients and how to develop and serve clients. They must be trained on the basic policies and procedures that will affect them immediately and in the future. Among the areas orientation training covers are:

- Where to get information
- How to use equipment
- How and when they get paid
- How to file or process medical claims

- Holidays and work schedules
- Key people and their role in the organization

Orientation training should also cover anything else they need to know to perform their job well and to feel comfortable within your organization. Some of these items are not readily apparent. For example, new employees need to be told about family members within your organization. In some family-owned businesses, divorced people work together or married people use their birth names.

Phase 2: Job related training

This is where the manager takes a new hire through all the key functions and key tasks of the position. The manager cannot assume that the new hire knows how to do all aspects of the job within acceptable quantity and quality standards. Generally, the need for this training is expressed by managers to candidates during the selection process.

Of course, the more experience the new hire has, the sooner this type of training will be completed. But no matter how experienced and skilled a new hire is, don't neglect job-related training. Do go through the entire group of key tasks. If not, you may later discover that key knowledge and skills are missing or have been forgotten, and poor habits have replaced good ones.

Phase 3: Continuous development

This is an underutilized training process in most organizations. Once top performers are developed, their knowledge is not requested, even though using this knowledge can lead to continuously improving techniques among many, if not all, employees.

Continuous development training can be a regularly scheduled meeting on a monthly basis facilitated by a manager. The manager asks a top producer to demonstrate a key skill or task to others. This training group is for all the people who perform that particular function or job. This training has high credibility among employees.

The trainer, the person who excels at the task or skill, is respected for his or her skill. The trainer gains recognition and prestige by sharing knowledge. ***The real knowledge and skill in any job is at the level of those currently performing at a top level,*** yet only a few organizations have a means of capturing top performers' knowledge and skill and passing them on to the whole team.

"The speed of the pack is determined
By the speed of the leader."
—Author unknown

Common errors in training programs

- **Giving too much information too soon**

When I first trained real estate agents, we had a workbook and two to three weeks of solid training that included the entire process of obtaining a property to sell and following up after the closing. It was great information, but too much knowledge with no specific action or participation.

- **Wrong person responsible for training**

Often smaller businesses have one person conducting all the training. In other words, training is centralized. For developmental tasks, it's much more effective to have the line managers in charge of training their team. Line managers are responsible and accountable for the job performance of the people under them. And only the line manager can easily combine concept, demonstration, role play, field assignment and tight feedback.

- **Failure to end each session with an action assignment**

Real training takes place when information is applied in the field and the event is recycled to determine what went well as well as what needs to be improved. Training is less than 10% retained if it isn't combined with action.

- **Failure to prepare and debrief a trainee before and after they do a task for the first time**

The greatest retention occurs when training is provided just before the trainee is about to perform the task. This was one of the missing pieces in my three weeks of training. But even more critical is the necessity of closing the loop by providing instant feedback the first time the new task is performed. Managers who debrief trainees after they perform a task for the first time will reinforce what worked and also identify any necessary changes in the trainee's technique.

- **Assuming a new hire is trained because of early strong performance**

This is a trap too many sales managers fall into. A new person goes partially through the job-related training and has early successes. Everyone senses this person is ready. Training ends. Two months later, this person's sales performance drops for no apparent reason. People like this are missing skills they performed earlier, but which were never reinforced. Or the new hire may be missing a key process that was never covered in training.

- **No tracking procedure to sign off on job-related training**

Use a job-related training outline listing the skills, knowledge, attitudes and habits for performing each job task. The list should also have a measurement of competency for each skill. The manager evaluates the trainee's competency and signs off when the skill level is adequate. I have included a sample Job-Related Training Outline at the back of this book.

- **Not staying on task until successful**

People need training as long as it takes to master the task or skill. Without training for mastery, the manager will fail to build a foundation for long-term success.

Traditional training methods

People learn in different ways. Not everyone will learn well from the primary training method you like to use. So, it's best to combine training methods or vary methods. Each training method has advantages and disadvantages.

- **Imitation:** This is best for people needing proof or credibility. It shows, in real time, the job being performed well. But imitation may threaten the trainee if too much is covered or if the style of the trainer is different that that of the trainee.

- **Experience:** Experience is the best teacher. But it takes time and can be costly. We all retain what we have learned through painful trial and error.

- **Lecture/tell:** With this training method, you can get lots of information out in a hurry. You can impress your audience with your knowledge. The downside is that only 5-10% of the information is retained and listening to a lecture can be boring. At best, the lecture method is like drinking water through a fire hose and should be only a small part of every training module.

How people really learn

Adult learners go through very predictable stages of learning until they develop habits. The goal of all training is to develop the good work habits—a combination of attitudes, skills and knowledge required to perform each job-related task. Think about how you learned to drive a car or a bicycle. When you think back, you will realize that you transitioned through these stages of learning:

- **Unconscious Incompetent:** In the beginning, you do not know what you don't know or, for that matter, what you do know. Here you are just beginning and maybe not very confident. The next two stages of learning happen simultaneously but need to be facilitated by a trainer.
- **Consciously Incompetent:** You become aware of what you do not know. A skillful trainer will take you through a process of self-discovery. This is a way for you to best own and retain what you learn.
- **Consciously Competent:** Here you become aware of the things you are doing well. But only through discovering their positive attributes will you reinforce and retain them as

habits. This is the most neglected aspect of development. Training often ends before this stage is complete.

- **Unconsciously Competent:** This where something performed well is natural. The employee performs the job skill like a gifted salesperson, professional athlete or world-class musician performs their well-honed craft. It's similar to how you suddenly arrive safely at your driving destination without remembering your every action.

An outline for successful training

Often trainees are taught how to do an important task but later fail to perform that task properly. I believe people need to know where their job and key tasks fit into the larger picture. Trainees are much more likely to learn, remember and apply their training when they know what will happen if the task is not performed properly. Learning increases when people understand the positive impact that doing their work well will have on their next task, as well as its impact on other workers and the company. This is where the insignificant becomes important.

As an example, in this book we have explained the impact and importance of selecting the right person for the right job. This process begins with defining the position. Without this key step, the other steps do not work! You could hire a terrific performer, but if you have not first defined the job and made sure you match each candidate's qualifications to that particular job, then your selection process will likely fail.

Before you begin any task training, ask your trainees why they think that a particular task is important. Make sure they know the value of doing the task well and how that task fits into the big picture. Ask them the long-term impact of not performing or poorly performing the task. By using this technique of ask-tell-ask, you ensure that the trainee understands the whys of performing this aspect of his job. Now he is ready and motivated to learn how to perform the task correctly.

Involve trainees through demonstration and role-play

Demonstrate the entire task for the trainees. Then ask them what they noticed. Next, break down the task into smaller logical steps. You do this first by demonstrating each step and again asking them what they observed and fielding all questions. Now have trainees role play the task. Once the task is completed, conduct a debriefing.

Debriefing is done by asking trainees what they did well. The trainer will respond last and always cite additional areas that were done correctly. Even with a poorly done role play, positives can be found. By engaging trainees in performing the task, you are using many learning styles and taking them through the stages of learning. Trainees then discuss what they need to do to improve. The trainer follows up with any other suggested areas of improvement. The last part of the training is the discussion of what the trainees learned. This should cover both the areas they did well and those requiring improvement.

As the trainer, your role is one of facilitation and engaging trainees. By doing this, you enable them to become consciously aware of where they are in the learning process. Repeat this exercise until the trainee or trainees are able to perform the entire task correctly. They'll learn some tasks quickly. Others may take several rounds of repetition. ***But here's the key: Only move on to a new task when you are certain trainees can correctly perform the current task.*** They should demonstrate that they can perform the task with an acceptable level of quality and within an acceptable time frame.

Assign application in field

Once trainees can role play the task successfully, have them perform that task in their daily work environment. Give them a specific task to perform within a period of time and ask them to get back to you (or their manager) with feedback on the project. Be specific about the task, the completion time and the meeting with the manager.

Feedback on field project

The trainees and trainer (manager) will close the loop on this field assignment. Use the same format for feedback:

> What worked?
> What needs to be done better?
> What did you learn?

Trainees always answer each question first (before the trainer.) If the task has been performed at an acceptable level of quality and quantity, the manager can note this task as completed and move on to the next.

You can use this same process for continuous training. The manager may be the *planner, training session leader and engager of the participants*. Ongoing training is optional training. Ensure that the participants know that if they attend, they must agree to share information, participate in the process and take action based on what they learn. Begin each new session with feedback on individual field actions. Close the loop on those actions and then develop the new material. Let the participants pick and prioritize the content of these training sessions. When I first utilized this process, I had the group develop a list and then prioritize the subjects that they wanted to review. This set the agenda, but more importantly, they took ownership of the agenda because they built it! Engage people in the development in order to build commitment to a process.

Getting the most from your training dollar

CEOs, owners and employees often attend training sessions at national conventions and trade association meetings. Typically, they receive good information but it's soon forgotten and almost certainly not implemented. Here's how to break that cycle.

Require that when anyone returns from a national convention where they attended breakout sessions or keynote addresses, they conduct debriefing and implementation workshops when they return in order to share and facilitate the implementation of what they learned. All convention attendees should also write a plan to implement the best ideas they picked up at the meeting. Knowledge is useless unless implemented.

CHAPTER 7

MANAGEMENT: A MEANS TO A DESIRED END

The complex process of management is simplified when you realize that you manage things (money, information other hard resources), but you also manage and lead people. The art is to understand how to use management information as a leadership tool for continuous growth and development.

Ultimately, you want your managers to become self-managed and to identify problems and turn them into opportunities. You want them to recognize and capitalize on opportunities. In great organizations, this becomes a fundamental understanding. Everyone shares the organization's vision and works together. Everyone also agrees upon objective means of measuring performance. This is particularly crucial in family-owned businesses.

Recall the way we defined management and leadership at the beginning of this book:

Management—the planning, developing, controlling and maximizing of information, resources, money, time and technology to achieve preset agreed upon objectives.

Leadership—the discovering, developing and empowering of people to achieve their personal goals while achieving the organization's goals.

Or think of management as the hard, objective side of success—the iron fist—with the power to get things done. Place that iron fist into the velvet glove of leadership. Leadership is the more subjective, motivational side of success. The iron fist in the velvet glove turns accountability into an environment of continuous improvement and learning.

At www.business-wise.com, we recommend and teach the Closed Loop Management Process, which promotes continuous learning.

Closed Loop Management

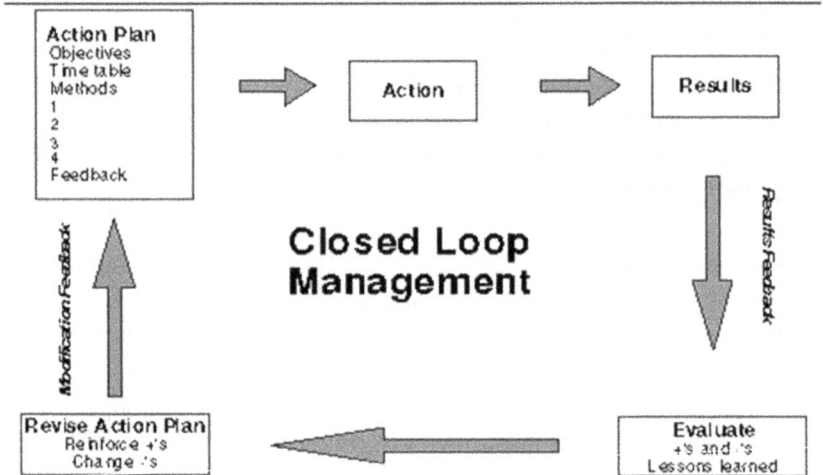

Take a minute to read and study this diagram. It's true that one picture or one diagram can be worth a thousand words.

The necessary ingredients to create closed loop management

Building a Closed Loop Process in your organization requires you to make several critical decisions. At first you will need to determine how to:

- Set meaningful goals
- Measure goal achievement

72

- Develop action plans to achieve goals
- Develop feedback systems
- Use feedback to promote growth and learning
- Conduct progress reviews toward goal achievement
- Revise and reinforce the business action plan

Do understand that your managers are the facilitators of the closed loop management process. They will define meaningful and measurable goals; develop sequenced actions for their achievement; set up mutually agreed upon feedback systems to evaluate progress; and perform all the other decisions and tasks that will make this process work. Together with your management team, you can turn the process into one of growth and continuous improvement. This makes your journey to goal achievement a significant experience for all.

Action plan development

Your organization's action plan is the statement of what you really desire to achieve. It's a written document stated in measurable terms. Action plans have three pathways of measurable performance: a Minimum Standard, an Expected Standard and a Maximized Standard of performance.

Why three pathways or ranges of performance? To avoid over management (micro management) and under management ("anything goes" style). By quantifying a low (minimum) and high (maximum) level of performance, your team leaders are obligated to intervene when performance nears either extreme of the pathway. This is much easier than using a single goal where there is a pass or fail system.

Minimum Standard of performance is not rewarded other than by retention in the position. Expected achievement is the old forecasted goal and it should remit average or modest rewards for its achievement. However, the Maximum Standard should be a reach. It should be achievable only with exceptional effort. When your organization reaches a maximized standard, employees should receive high rewards for that accomplishment.

A timetable defines when each goal is to be achieved. Include a list of sequential steps that will lead to each goal. Have check-points along the way to let you know if you are on target. For example, if the 12-month goal is to increase revenue by $5 million, you might have quarterly steps: in the first three months, revenues will increase $1.25 million; second three months by $2.5 million; and the third quarter by $3.75. These check-points or feedback points must be agreed upon by the leadership team.

> *"Make good habits and they will make you."*
> —*Parks Cousins*

Feedback rules

- Feedback needs to be meaningful to both the giver and the receiver of feedback
- Feedback needs to be quantitative whenever possible
- Feedback should be easy to give and receive: the process should be accurate, time efficient and easy to retrieve
- Feedback needs to be timely as well as relevant
- No feedback assumes no activity
- There must be feedback on the feedback—acknowledgement that it has been received and relevant comments rendered by the receiver
- False feedback is grounds for dismissal

The difficulty in managing

Let's stop for a minute and talk about management. It's a tough job. Many managers feel like they don't know how to manage. Or they're not comfortable holding people accountable. Some managers think they don't have the time to manage others well. They complain about having poor performers on their team or having a lack of expectations from senior officers. A lack of training, a fear of rejection—you name it and it's probably been used as an excuse for why managing is so difficult. But adhering to the closed loop diagram and the action plan can overcome most of these objections.

Too often plans are made and then not reviewed in a manner that allows for learning and growth. The concept of the journey being more important than the goal becomes a reality with a good leadership process like the closed loop. Help only works when performance is improved in a manner that allows both the helper and those being helped to learn and grow personally. This closed loop process fosters input and contributions from all. That in turn enhances self-worth and value for each individual and the group or team, which also leads to a reduction in the perception that management is difficult.

The Closed Loop Process: A process of continuous improvement

So in four easy steps, here is an explanation of how the Closed Loop Process can provide your organization with a way to continually improve and continually move closer to its ultimate vision.

Step 1:
Develop your action plan
- Establish quantifiable objectives and obtain agreement on those objectives
- Set the timetable for achievement
- Develop the key methods or actions to reach all objectives in logical sequence
- Define early feedback (check-points on progress)

When you develop the action plan with all these elements, you're beginning to avoid the trap of Management By Crisis (MBC). MBC is when all you do is continuously bounce between action and results, putting out fires in reaction mode. Without the ability to plan, meet a timetable and reach objectives, reaction management rules the day. Certainly, without an action plan there is no opportunity for continuous improvement. .

Step 2:
Take action: To make things happen, action needs to take place. Most successful owners are excellent at taking action. Instill in your management team the need to act every day in ways that will bring the company closer to those agreed upon goals and objectives.

Step 3:
Deal with the results of actions: What you do with the results of your actions is critical for creating an atmosphere of learning and continuous improvement. Managers and leaders are developed in the next step as they learn to think critically and engage team members to recognize not only success, but also problems.

Step 4:
Evaluate, adjust and continue: Here's the key to leadership. Compare what you planned to have happen (from your action plan) with the feedback from actual results. First examine what worked well in your plan and what adjustments you made consciously to your plan when implementing. Then review what in the plan did not work or was not implemented. Finally, sum up key points from what worked well, as well as what did not, and decide on what you will reinforce because of its positive impact. Decide what changes you will implement to make your plan and results more favorable. This is the same process we used in training and would be the same process used for formal performance reviews. Understand and implement the Closed Loop Process and you will become a better leader and developer of talent.

Closed Loop Process success story

Example 1
A large U.S. based personnel consulting firm was a long-time client of BusinessWise. The firm had no management or leadership development process. After working with them for three plus years, we implemented the Closed Loop Process as a follow up on our annual planning process. At the quarterly management meeting, each manager closed the loop on the last quarter and ultimately

shared the corrective actions made, as well as his or her successes. Each team member received a report prior to the quarterly management meeting. The participants read each report and were prepared to ask the reporting manager questions and share what they liked. This process taught managers to self-manage. After each manager reported, individual managers offered inputs and shared what they learned. Managers became better leaders as these real life experiences were shared and as they received advice from their peers. Management and leadership skills were honed by a process of continuous improvement. The organization was able to prosper and attract talent because the environment engaged people to learn.

Example 2
A printing firm was progressive and growing, but they were not as profitable as they wanted to be. We closed the loop on how work flowed through the company and discovered several hundreds of dollars in spoiled jobs. We developed a plan to solve this issue, which included work flow and sign-off procedures from sales to prepress. We set up a communication plan with suggested procedures and an incentive program where the staff would share in the savings. Monthly, the teams met and closed the loop on their work flow and added improvements suggested by their teams; management met quarterly just to review their progress. The blaming stopped and they dropped more than $300K to the bottom line profits after bonuses were paid to employees.

The closed loop process engages people and provides an opportunity for people to be appreciated. It is human nature to want to be a valued part of an organization and be part of a learning and growth environment. A simple reproducible leadership-management process like the Closed Loop could transform your organization.

CHAPTER 8

MOTIVATION: THE MOST SOPHISTICATED MANAGEMENT FUNCTION

Motivation is a misunderstood role in management and leadership. Too many business owners believe and act as if leadership must do something to or for someone in order to motivate that person. The truth is motivation comes from within.

Motivation is deep within us and it's the reason why we want something. Most leadership success in the area of motivation comes from doing things *with* rather than *to* or *for* someone. Your role as a manager or leader is to provide an atmosphere where positive motivation takes place. This is crucial. Most turnover of top talent occurs due to a lack of an atmosphere for positive motivation.

What doesn't motivate

So, if you want to motivate people you must avoid these two common pitfalls.

• Doing for
When you try to motivate people by doing something *for* them, you fail to develop stronger talent and you build dependency needs. An example would be, a sales manger giving a salesperson a lead or closing a sale rather than developing the skills with the salesperson and teaching him to fish and feed himself for life.

• Doing to

When a leader tries to motivate by doing something *to* people (carrot and stick approach), people interpret the action as punitive. This type of leader fails to recognize that motives are individual and deep.

> *"Leaders create energy in others*
> *by instilling purpose."*
>
> —*Author unknown*

The manager's/leader's role in the motivational process

The main role we have in motivating people is in establishing and nurturing the right environment. We have already begun to develop a positive motivational environment if we have hired, trained and developed people properly. Each process previously discussed in this book is a key step in building a positive motivational atmosphere or environment.

The motivational environment

Essentially, there are three major areas that make up the motivational environment at the workplace. You need to establish the first two areas in order to earn the right to access the third and most powerful motivational area.

1. Job Fit

Each member of the team, including the team leader, needs to be a good fit for his position and to be experiencing job success and performance. Each person needs to be engaged in his role and to be meeting or exceeding expectations. A well selected and well functioning employee needs to exist before the other key elements of a positive motivational environment can be achieved.

2. Functioning Team

This is a common job objective for every leader and manager: *To build a team capable of achieving the unit's goals, while also achieving each member's goals.* This is the classic win-win environment. Here are the key characteristics of a high functioning team:

- **Established and agreed upon roles:** Each member has a defined role and offers something unique and significant to the team's success
- **One team leader:** There is one leader who is responsible for building this team to achieve its goals. This person is the center of the business universe.
- **Reasonable span of control:** Normally, leaders should have no more than five to eight direct reports. This depends on the complexity of the team goals and roles of team members. If the business universe becomes too large, sub-groups within the team develop and team effectiveness is diminished.
- **Shared goals and values:** It's essential that the goals of the team are shared and agreed upon and that common expectations among team members are clear.
- **Interdependency:** On an effective team, talents are diverse and the roles are different. Each team member is made stronger because he or she can depend on the other members to perform their role and job.
- **Mutual response bonds:** A strong team does not have one-way interaction from leader down to individual team members. And dialog isn't limited to individual discussions between the leader and individual team members. Strong teams have multiple interactions among all team members.
- **Trust and respect:** There may be differences in personalities and beliefs, but there is respect for those differences. Everyone contributes in his or her unique manner and skill set. Trust is high among all team members that they will fulfill their role and commitments as they share many common values and the team goals.
- **Strong communications:** There should be clear direction, understood roles and a minimum of surprises. The abundance of mutual response bonds further clarifies communications. This means that team members interact

with each other and build stronger relationships. Ideas, inputs and contributions from every member are respected.

- **Synergy:** *The* sum is greater than all of the individual members in a high functioning team. 1 + 1 + 1 +1 = 8

Take a minute to evaluate your own team. How does it stack up against these key characteristics? Are there areas of real strengths that you can further maximize?

3. Personal Goals

This third major area of the motivational environment is key. You must first establish job fit and a well functioning team before you can earn the right to access this most powerful motivational area. It's the most sophisticated aspect of leadership.

Understand that people do not work for the sake of work. They work for what the results of their job will allow them to do personally. People are truly engaged when the job is a vehicle to achieving their personal goals. Conversely, you probably know of good employees who left an organization because they no longer felt their goals could be achieved in their work. Look for the opportunity to learn about your team member's personal goals and try to develop a way that they can achieve them in your environment while the unit achieves its goal.

Here is an example. I conducted an organizational study of a retail lumber and home supply store. Our study identified a part-time worker who was highly respected and had the talent to become a general manager. He had worked in the store from high school through college. The owner wanted to hire him full time as his number two person behind the CEO. This person had a strong interest in body building and coaching and when first approached for the general manager's position, he declined.

He thought if he accepted, he would lose the ability to pursue his workouts and coaching. I advised the owner to conduct an interview to dig a little deeper with the candidate and to determine if there was an opportunity to have him achieve his goals while working as a general manager. Through some flextime and strong performance indicators for the store, the person accepted the position and led the company to record performances for ten years. A win-win was reached by listening and determining that there was a way to satisfy the business and personal goals.

Key learning

Personal goals drive many business decisions. It happens with owners and family members, managers and strong producers. Earn the right to access your team members' personal goals and construct ways for your talented people to achieve their goals in your business environment. Do it annually in a separate meeting where you discuss only what is important to them.

CHAPTER 9

SUCCESSION PLANNING: THE CEO'S MOST NEGLECTED RESPONSIBILITY

Many attorneys, when they help set up a business' legal structure, urge business founders to establish how they will transfer or end the business ownership at the same time. This makes sense. *Because when you're forming the business, all parties are reasonable and unemotional*.

The reason you need a succession plan is in case of your untimely death or illness or, even more likely, in case you become bored with the day-to-day business operation. The last reason, in my experience, is prevalent with successful owners. Family businesses are often a large portion of the owners' estate and will require many issues to be discussed among family members and the owners. These issues include:

- Fairness to all family members
- Ability of family members to operate the business
- Objectivity in all decisions
- Legal documents to allow the owners' exit
- Tax considerations
- A funding mechanism to allow succession
- A succession communication plan

Succession options

As an owner, you have several major options:

1. Sell the entity to a third party outside of the business.
2. Sell to family members running the business.
3. Sell to an existing internal management team.
4. Retention of the business within the family as a long-term investment
5. Conduct a systematic liquidation of assets.
6. Allow the owner to die on the job without any succession plan.

All of the options require proactive planning except this last option. This option isn't a good one. Avoid it.

Certain practices need to change when you move into succession preparation. Early in the business cycle, when the owners begin to earn a high income, their strategy includes minimizing taxes. This lowers reportable income. But when owners are preparing for a sale or transition of their business, they need to maximize profits, which may require higher taxes and audited financial statements for several years.

Create your succession plan long before you need it

Also, in order to make a more prompt exit, the owner needs to have depth in leadership and management. Leadership depth enables the business to run profitably without the owner's day-to-day presence.

Many owners think that the succession plan can be very quickly put together and an orderly sale can take place within a year or eighteen months. This assumption is incorrect. Depending on some of the issues we have discussed, it could take two to five years. To create the most options and build the highest possible value for your business, start your succession plan long before you need it. There are people issues: do I have the right leadership talent in place to run the business when I am gone? How do I handle family members in or out of the business? What are the tax ramifications of my plan? What reporting must be changed to show greatest value? Will the buyer want my real estate? How much money do I need to maintain my current life style? Will I stay on board with the new owner? As you can see, a successful transition cannot be done overnight.

Key parts of every plan

The three essential parts of succession planning are: people, finances and legal. The most neglected piece is people. Choosing the right person or people to transfer the business to is a judgment that financial consultants, legal advisors and many owners are not equipped to make. But good judgment here will grant the owners more personal options. Poor judgment on the people portion of succession planning will be the downfall of any succession plan.

Begin the process of succession planning by initiating communication among the owners, family members and key management. First, let's look at the family business and its succession with regard to people issues.

Family-owned businesses: The planning process is more complicated

Compared to other privately owned businesses, family-owned businesses present more challenges when you try to create an ownership succession plan. Much of the complication boils down to roles. There are multiple roles a family member may have in a family-owned business:

- **Family Member:** This is a role separate from a business role and a family member may assume other roles related to the business or not.
- **Owner:** In this role, you could be a board member and have a proportionate share only in the net profits.
- **Management:** Here you are actively engaged as an operational leader and most likely you are an owner or anticipate being an owner. You could be an owner and a manager working for a senior manager who is a nonowner.
- **Employee:** You could be an employee and owner working for a family member who is a manager and also an owner. It is also possible you could be working as an employee/owner for a manager who is a not a family member or an owner.

As you can see, it is important that you understand your role at a particular time and place and act accordingly. Some family businesses have certain rules to follow in these instances. For example, a family might not discuss family issues at work and avoid discussing work issues at family gatherings. In more sophisticated family businesses where there are strong objective selection processes in place, a family member assumes a business role only if he or she meets objective requirements and fits the position. This value system can prevent family members from being placed in jobs for which they aren't qualified. Compensation needs to be objective for family members and based on the position and performance in that position.

In a family business, many processes need to be in place to assure long-term success from generation to generation. These considerations must include:

- Fairness to family members and employees
- Preparation of family members to "fit" positions in the organization
- Compensation based on job performance
- Processes that assure objectivity in all the above areas

Most of all, the owners must agree to be objective and "willing to let go" of their leadership role. Communication is essential to the entire business transferal or business succession process. The following is a process that I have facilitated with owners. I've also used this process with my partners. It's based on the fact that many business decisions are driven by unarticulated personal goals. The process described below will only work where there is respect and trust among all the participants. It is advised that a professional facilitator be used.

How to start the "letting go" process

You need all parties to agree to the three criteria as a basis to begin a discussion for a successful transfer of a family-owned business from one generation to the next:

1. Agreement by all stakeholders that the survival, growth and perpetuation of the business is paramount.
2. Agreement to honor personal goals as long as those goals don't conflict with step one.
3. Ability to compromise. Compromise is always necessary but will be lessened if you follow steps one and two.

All participants in the succession planning discussion must agree with the items above. If they do not, this process can't go forward successfully. This works *only* when there's a foundation of mutual respect and trust.

I developed this process for a client when one owner wanted to buy the other's stock. They could not go through this discussion on their own because it was too painful. Yet, I realized there was a mutual respect and fondness between the partners. This process took me six months to develop and was the basis for a successful transition. The owners trusted me and had a high regard for each other, which allowed the process to work. There must be a respectful relationship in place to allow the process to work. As founders of the business, they had to agree that the survival and growth of the business must be preserved. It is always sound to have a common basis of values to use as a standard to check goals.

As the parties shared their personal and business goals through a facilitated discussion and they realized the goals were congruent with the long-term survival and growth of the organization, they discovered that their personal goals were more likely to be actualized. The participants maintained an atmosphere of acceptance and validity for each other's goals. As the process continued, they both realized that their goals could be accomplished once shared and understood. At the very end, there was a willingness to develop a set of standards and a process for exploring a mutually satisfactory buy-out of a partner. With all the work done up front, the attorney had only to develop an agreement that reflected their mutual understanding. The sale was consummated and the partners remained friends, and the business moved forward offering more opportunity to key management.

A potential win-win became a lose-lose

Here's an example of what not to do. After several very successful years in my real estate business, I discussed with my partner my personal goal to become a management consultant. I wanted to work with a consulting organization that had been very instrumental in our success as business owners. My partner at that time, instead of asking why that was important to me, ridiculed my goal.

You might say this was not our closest moment Our relationship was never the same after that. We parted ways about two years later. I sold the real estate business to one of my managers and accomplished my goal of becoming a management consultant. If my partner and I had an appreciation for the process and ground rules that we are reviewing in this chapter, our discussion may have taken a different turn. We would have explored what needed to be done in the business for me to become a management consultant. That could have developed a win-win scenario for my partner and me rather than the ultimate lose-lose scenario.

> *"One of the tests of leadership is the ability to recognize a problem before it becomes an emergency."*
> —*Arnold Glasgow*

In another true story, three owners were offered a sizable amount of money for their business. (Although I had often suggested that they go through a process of sharing personal goals as a prelude to the past planning meetings, they had always been unwilling). In the end, they could not agree upon terms of an offer that would best meet their unarticulated personal and business goals. Certain unexpressed personal goals were driving their respective decisions. Instead of working together, the two major partners independently explored several transition alternatives. The best alternative was not accepted because of a sticking point that appeared to give one partner a preferred position rather than one of equality. As a result, they missed their opportunity, although both parties wanted to be cashed out. They took a less desirable alternative that did not meet their personal goals. The market place changed and their business was substantially devalued and their desired exit deferred well into the future. They are now prisoners of their own business.

ACTION PLAN FOR GOAL DISCUSSION

1. Get agreement on ground rules:
   a. Survival, growth and perpetuation of the business are paramount.
   b. Personal goals should be honored as long as the first criteria (A) is not at risk.
   c. Need to compromise will be less if A and B are followed.

2. Sharing of personal and business goals process:
   a. Each participant prepares his or her own list of personal and business goals.
   b. Take turns sharing goals.
   c. Do not place personal judgment on the worthiness of any else's goal(s).
   d. To assure understanding, one owner may question what another means by his or her goal. This may result in the restatement of the goal.
   e. The participants are asked if they would like this goal to be achieved. If the goal is accepted by all, the process starts again with a different person sharing his or her goal.
   f. If the goal is not accepted, there is a brief discussion of what may not be acceptable and perhaps restated as a clarified goal. If the amended goal is accepted, the process starts over with a new goal being shared.
   g. Unaccepted goals are placed on a separate sheet for later discussion.
   h. This process continues until all of the goals have been shared.

Many personal goals can be met through the business

Through this process, you may discover a few surprises. But many personal goals, once shared and understood, can be met through the accomplishment of business goals.

This process fosters synergism. It's a foundation for an enhanced win-win environment. With most business succession plans, there are only one or two goals that need to be worked out. Abiding by this structure will give you the right atmosphere to encourage open discussion and compromise without jeopardizing the survival and growth of your organization.

I have used this process as the first step in initiating a business planning retreat. That way, the owners and key senior managers enter the retreat knowing each other's personal goals. This allows for a freer and safer discussion of business goals and implementation alternatives. Every time I've done this, the retreat environment has been charged with positive expectations.

CHAPTER 10

ANALYSIS OF YOUR BUSINESS UNIVERSE

I have given you a lot to think about as a business owner. It's now time to look at your direct reports and, based on some of the concepts you have read about in this book, perform an analysis of your business universe.

Your business universe consists of your direct reports. Our analysis will determine where you stand as a team of business leaders and managers and how you can (through this team) assure that your organization will survive, sustain continuous profitable growth and perpetuate itself beyond your lifetime or interest span. This is the first step in building a stronger organization. This is a hard look at the primary leadership team and its dynamic qualities.

Evaluate your personal business universe

The criteria for evaluating your direct reports are: performance, communication and shared values. At BusinessWise, we've developed this eight-step process:

1. Rate each direct report on a scale of 0-3 in each category (performance, communication and shared values). The higher the numerical score, the better the rating. The best rating is a total of 9. On the next page are two copies of a form you can use for this purpose.
2. Place a dot in the center of a clean piece of paper representing you as the center of this business universe.

3. Draw a short line toward 12:00 o'clock from that dot to the name of the person with the highest score. (This is the person closest to you.)

4. Draw a much longer line from you to 6:00 o'clock and write the name of the person with the lowest score there. This line will be the longest and connects you with the person furthest from you.

5. Around your dot, continue to write the names of your direct reports and draw a line connecting each to you, making the length of line representative of the strength of their score. Shorter lines mean higher scores and closer connections to you.

6. Draw a circle that represents an acceptable culture score equidistant from you as the center. People inside the circle have acceptable scores in all three areas: performance, communication and values. You may consider any score of 0 or 1 in any area to place a person automatically outside of the acceptable culture line.

7. Examine who is inside the culture line and who is outside. Problem-solve with direct reports outside the culture line to determine what you need to do to bring them into stronger connection with you and the team.

8. Take corrective action where appropriate and use your best relationships as potential benchmarks for future selection criteria.

BUSINESS UNIVERSE EVALUATION FORM

Direct Report's Name _____

Date _____

Rate this direct report on a scale of 1-3 in each criterion.
1 = Poor
2 = Average
3 = Good

Criteria

Job Performance	
Communication Skills	
Shared Values with You & Team	

CHAPTER 11

POTENTIAL ACTIONS

Congratulations. By reading through this book, you have already demonstrated your commitment to building a great organization. We have covered a lot of information. You should now have some clear actions that you can take.

If you are overwhelmed as a company owner and not sure where to start, you may want to seek professional assistance from an experienced business management consultant.

How do you eat an elephant? You know this: One bite at a time! You may want to reread parts of this book and work on one issue at a time. Here are some suggestions to get you started on the path toward building a great organization.

- Complete the business universe analysis (Chapter 10). What did you learn from it? What actions should you take?
- In what stage of growth are you? Are you prepared for it, and also for the next stage of growth?
- How deep is your leadership team? How can you make it deeper?
- How well do you perform the elements of the CEO position as described in Chapter 3? Rate each area discussed from 1 to 5 with a score of 5 meaning you are fully competent in that area. Commit to improve.
- How good is your leadership development program? You have been exposed to sample systems for obtaining and selecting talent; training and development of all employees;

the continuous development process; and developing a positive motivational environment. How well are these processes working?

- What is your succession plan? If you don't have one, reread Chapter 9 and start building one.

Take action-make a decision to Build a Great Organization- You now know the Secrets and where you can begin.

Pick one or two areas and write out a simple action plan using the form on the next page. Then, do it.

"Knowledge without action is useless and a terrible waste of knowledge and time. Action without knowledge is dangerous."

—Author Unknown

Call the author, Bruce G. Clinton, to arrange a free consultation if you have identified areas where you need input. Call 203.458.1219 or email: bclinton@business-wise.com

Objective: (What outcome do you want?) Make your objective specific, measurable, achievable and realistic.

_____

_____

_____

_____

Timetable: (By what date will you accomplish this objective?)

_____

Methods: (What sequential steps will you take to achieve your objective?)

1. _____

2. _____

3. _____

4. _____

5. _____

6. _____

Feedback: (What checkpoints will you use to determine if you are on target to achieve your goal on time?)

1. _____

2. _____

3. _____

4. _____

5. _____

6. _____

DATE: _____

BOOK FEEDBACK

Your feedback on this book, *The Secrets Of Building A Great Organization*, is vitally important to BusinessWise and author Bruce Clinton. We value and appreciate any comments you're willing to share.

Name: _____

Positon: _____

Address: _____

Phone: _____

Email: _____

1.   What is your most significant personal gain from this book?

2.   Please indicate your overall reaction to this book.

Excellent ( )   Good ( )   Average ( )   Fair ( )

3.   What is the likelihood that you will apply lessons learned from this book?

Excellent ( )   Good ( )   Average ( )   Fair ( )

4.   In your opinion, what were some of the most helpful features of the book?

5.   I am interested in a private, confidential, free, no obligation discussion.

Yes( )   No( )

6. Other Comments:

Email this feedback form to bclinton@business-wise.com and receive our free blog information and future articles to help you to grow a Great Organization www.thefamilybusinessblog.com or follow join our Family Business Network on LinkedIn:

http://www.linkedin.com/groupRegistration?gid=2568529 .

ABOUT THE AUTHOR

BRUCE G. CLINTON

Bruce G. Clinton is the founder of BusinessWise, LLC, a Connecticut-based executive coaching and consulting firm that specializes in helping entrepreneurial organizations solve strategic problems associated with growth and transition. Bruce is also co-founder of ASearch, LLC, a retained executive search firm that takes a unique organizational development approach to finding key people, removing the risk and doubt from hiring key people.

His expertise in organization and management development derives from more than 35 years as a consultant. He's in demand as a seminar leader on management and leadership skill development. Among the many national conventions at which Bruce has delivered presentations addressing business owners are: the National Association of Personnel Services, the National Associations of Medical Equipment Suppliers and the National Association of Electrical Distributors.

Prior to becoming a management consultant, Bruce owned and built a multi office residential real estate company and was a general partner in a limited partnership, Heatherwood Associates, which developed 96 high end residential lots. He was also a co-owner of a residential construction company. He was a client of a consulting company which he later joined because of the success he experienced in developing managers and growing his real estate offices.

Bruce served as president of Organizational Development Associates, Inc. He is the cofounder of Entrepreneurial Resource Group, Inc., and the founder of Entrepreneurial Leadership Councils— peer groups of business owners who share the common desire to build strong organizations.

Bruce's clients have included companies in all sectors of business and industry, including many family owned businesses, all over the United States. He served human resource, insurance, real estate brokerage and development companies, as well as, durable medical equipment distributors, manufacturers, professional practices and nonprofit organizations.

Bruce is a graduate of Hobart College with a dual major of Economics and Psychology. He completed his MBA program at the University of New Haven; is a recipient of RCC and CBC (Registered Corporate Coach and Certified Business Coach) designations; served as a commissioned Air Force Officer; and has been an incorporator of a bank and past President of the Madison Country Club.

Bruce has served on the boards of various business and civic organizations. He currently serves as a board member of The Cove, a nonprofit organization that helps children and their families through the loss of a loved one. He and his wife, Susan, have five children and ten grandchildren.

ADDITIONAL RESOURCES

On the next few pages, you'll find two tools that have helped other organizations build toward greatness. These are samples of the types of articles you will receive if you complete the feedback on this book and indicate you would like to receive articles to help you grow your business

SELECTION INTERVIEW TACTICS

1. The day before the interview:
   - Review the job application
   - Block out 15 minutes before the interview and 30 minutes after it
   - Review your interview guide or questions you will ask
     - Will your list of questions tell you what you need to know about the candidate's ability to perform the job?
   - Make sure everything you'll need will be available (room, application, evaluation forms, etc.)

2. Use the 15 minutes before the job interview to:
   - Make a final review of the completed application
   - Check any material you want the applicant to take home
   - Make sure the room is in order and your materials are prepared
   - Get into a proper interviewing mindset
     - Remind yourself to see the person as he or she really is
     - Remind yourself to hire based on the candidate's past experience and ability to do the job at hand

3. Be on time for the interview. This sets a professional tone and helps avoid unnecessary hurrying.

4. Greet the applicant and start the interview immediately.

5. Follow your interview guide. When you use the same guide for each applicant, you can easily compare candidates. You also can make sure you cover all the essentials.

6. Give the applicant time to answer your questions and think. The applicant should do the majority of the talking.

7. Practice good listening skills.
- Don't be afraid of silence
- Use a nod of your head or smile at appropriate times (rather than speaking)
- Don't interrupt or complete sentences for the applicant
- Ask a question and stay silent until the applicant indicates he or she has completed the answer
- Repeat back to applicants key parts of important statements they make

8. Make frequent use of how and why questions.

9. Ask only one question at a time.

10. Phrase your question in simple language. Avoid jargon.

11. Phrase your questions so they are neutral. This means not indicating what type of response you're looking for. (Example: Don't say, "I imagine you were among the sales leaders in your company, right?" Do say: "How did you do in sales?")

12. Get the applicant to define terms and to speak in specifics. A general answer like, "I performed well at that task" needs to be explained in more measurable terms.

13. Move from general questions to specific questions.

14. Don't express your interpretation of what the applicant has said.

15. Probe but do not urge.

16. Take good notes.

17. Maintain control so you can get through all your questions.

JOB RELATED TRAINING OUTLINE

Job Title_____

Trainee_____ Company_____

Manager_____

Training began _____ Training ended _____

FUNCTION	TASKS	STANDARDS	COMPLET-ED	KNOWLEDGE	ATTITUDES	SKILLS	HABITS
Recruit excellent people for own team; develop a steady flow of candidates	*Develop job standards *Conduct Sphere of Influence calls *Conduct candidate contact call	Job Standard sent in for each job Leads after 5 calls: M S E 3 4 5 Candidates in funnel after 5 contacts: M S E 3 4 5		What job requirements are necessary for success Behavioral requirements for job Sources of Sphere of Influences	Patient Curious Committed Controlled enthusiasm	Development of action plans Develop fact benefits worksheet Communication skills	Recruit on regular basis Use total process Review process before taking next step
Select excellent people for own team	1. Conduct initial screening interview 2.Administer forms 3.Conduct exit interviews	S and I calls per week: M S E 1 3 5		Company Selection process Policy & procedures	Disciplined to use process	Sales skills Sales by objective	Compare candidate with essential behavior needed for job success
Post interview codes 7.3 or above—fit job and team	4. Check employer references 5. Check character references 6. Validate profile 7. Conduct comprehensive candidate interview 8. Conduct spouse interview 9. Conduct hiring expectations interview	Profile coded 7 or above in 5 oppor-tunities: M S E 3 4 5 Spouse interviews 5 opportunities: M S E 3 4 5		Qualifications of S and I Fact benefits or company & opportunity What profiles will & won't do Objectives of each step in process Feedback systems built into process Candidate philosophy		Planning & evaluation skills Interviewing & questioning skills How to develop sequenced questions	Close loop at the end of each call or step in the process Go for complete information and specifics Exit candidates early when they don't fit Use of feedback systems to your manager Take time necessary to do each step

q

www.ingramcontent.com/pod-product-compliance
Lightning Source LLC
Chambersburg PA
CBHW071505200326
41519CB00019B/5881